Outdoor Hunting Guide

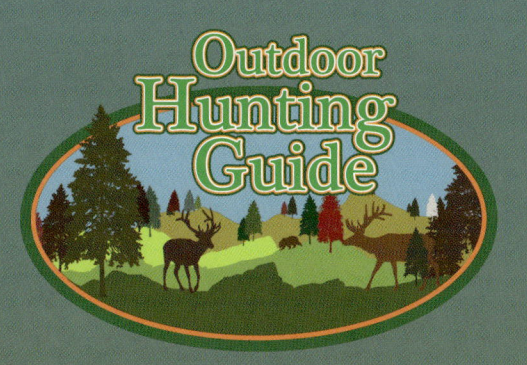

Birds

Pamela McDowell

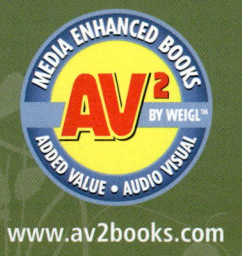

AV² provides enriched content that supplements and complements this book. Weigl's AV² books strive to create inspired learning and engage young minds in a total learning experience.

Your AV² Media Enhanced books come alive with...

Audio
Listen to sections of the book read aloud.

Key Words
Study vocabulary, and complete a matching word activity.

Video
Watch informative video clips.

Quizzes
Test your knowledge.

Embedded Weblinks
Gain additional information for research.

Slide Show
View images and captions, and prepare a presentation.

Try This!
Complete activities and hands-on experiments.

... and much, much more!

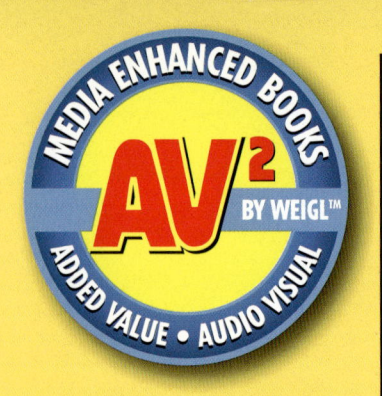

Go to www.av2books.com, and enter this book's unique code.

BOOK CODE

F613489

AV² by Weigl brings you media enhanced books that support active learning.

Published by AV² by Weigl
350 5th Avenue, 59th Floor
New York, NY 10118
Website: www.weigl.com   www.av2books.com

Copyright ©2013 AV² by Weigl.
All rights reserved. No part of this publication may be reproduced, stored in a retrieval system, or transmitted in any form or by any means, electronic, mechanical, photocopying, recording, or otherwise, without the prior written permission of the publisher.

Library of Congress Cataloging-in-Publication Data

McDowell, Pamela.
  Birds / Pamela McDowell.
     p. cm.
  Includes bibliographical references and index.
  ISBN 978-1-61913-505-5 (hard cover : alk. paper) — ISBN 978-1-61913-509-3 (soft cover : alk. paper) — ISBN 978-1-61913-700-4 (ebook)
 1. Fowling—Juvenile literature. I. Title.
 SK315.M33 2013
 799.2'4—dc23
                       2012005577

Printed in the United States of America in North Mankato, Minnesota
1 2 3 4 5 6 7 8 9   16 15 14 13 12

062012
WEP170512

Project Coordinator: Aaron Carr
Art Director: Terry Paulhus

Every reasonable effort has been made to trace ownership and to obtain permission to reprint copyright material. The publishers would be pleased to have any errors or omissions brought to their attention so that they may be corrected in subsequent printings.

Weigl acknowledges Getty Images as its primary image supplier for this title.

Outdoor Hunting Guide

Birds

Contents

2 AV² Book Code
4 What Is Bird Hunting?
6 Focus on Game Birds
8 History
10 Tracking
12 Equipment and Clothing
14 Safety
16 Hunting Responsibly
18 The Rules
20 After the Hunt
21 Game Bird Report
22 Take Aim Quiz
23 Key Words/Index
24 Log on to www.av2books.com

What Is Bird Hunting?

Hunting is pursuing animals in nature. People hunt animals for food or sport. Some hunters choose to search for birds. Bird hunting is sometimes called fowling. The birds people hunt are called game birds. These birds include turkeys, pheasants, quail, geese, and ducks.

Bird hunting is good exercise. A bird hunter must enjoy spending many hours outdoors. Game birds may be found near lakes and ponds or in deep **brush**. Some types of game birds live in rocky areas or around farm fields. Hunters learn about many different **habitats**. People who hunt also learn how to identify different kinds of birds.

Hunting birds can be a fun way to spend time with family and friends. There are clubs for bird hunters, and bird hunting is also practiced as a competitive sport. Sometimes, bird hunters use bows and arrows, but more often they use guns. A hunter safety course must be completed before a person can get a hunting license in most U.S. states and Canadian provinces.

Track the FACTS

- In the United States, 12.5 million people ages 16 and older hunted in 2006. Of those, 91 percent were male and 9 percent were female.
- That same year, 2.3 million people hunted birds such as ducks.
- People from age 6 to age 15 make up about 2 percent of hunters.

Birds 5

Focus on Game Birds

There are two types of birds that are hunted, and they are known by their habitats. Game birds that live on land are called upland birds. They are mainly hunted for food. Small upland game birds include pheasants, quail, and grouse. They weigh less than 4 pounds (1.8 kilograms). The male pheasant, called a rooster, has colorful feathers and a long tail. It is sometimes stuffed and kept as a **trophy**. States and provinces have different laws about when upland birds can be hunted, but most hunting seasons are between September and January. Wild turkeys, which are larger, may be hunted in the spring as well.

The other type of game bird is waterfowl. Ducks and geese are waterfowl. They live on lakes, ponds, or rivers, and they **migrate** as the seasons change. Waterfowl are hunted in early fall in the northern United States and Canada. This is when the birds begin to fly south for the winter. The hunting season is later in the fall in the southern United States.

Most waterfowl are hunted for food. A Canada goose may weigh from 8 to 12 pounds (3.6 to 5.4 kg). Ducks weigh much less, usually 2 to 3 pounds (0.9 to 1.4 kg).

The bobwhite quail is one of many kinds of quail in North America.

Game Birds

Pheasant

Pheasants live in open areas with low brush for cover. They are found throughout North America but are most common in the U.S. Midwest.

Teal

The teal lives in wetlands surrounded by plants. Teal are found mostly in the U.S. Midwest and Canadian Prairie provinces.

Dove

The dove lives in open wooded areas, near farms, and in deserts. Doves are found in most U.S. states and in southern Canada.

Canada Goose

Canada geese live near lakes, bays, and fields. This waterfowl has a black head and neck, with white patches on its face. Canada geese are mainly found in the northern United States and Canada.

Mallard

The mallard is considered a waterfowl. Mallards live near marshes, ponds, and lakes. They are found in most U.S. states and in many parts of western Canada. These ducks are often called greenheads.

In the 1800s, game birds were traded at the North American posts of the Hudson's Bay Company.

History

People have hunted for survival throughout history. Native Peoples in North America hunted birds with bows and arrows. They also trapped birds. People living in deserts hunted the kind of quail that live in hot climates. These birds were often easy to find and catch. Quail was cooked over an open fire. The bird's feathers were sewn onto clothing used in special ceremonies. The quail became a character in many stories passed down by desert people.

Hunting methods changed when Europeans brought firearms to North America. In the 1600s, settlers used **muzzle-loaded** guns to hunt waterfowl. Shotguns became popular in the late 1800s. The first shotguns had a **range** of only 25 yards (23 meters). After improvements were made, hunters could fire farther and could take more shots without reloading.

Birds were an important food source for the early European settlers on the eastern coast of North America. Some of these settlers made a living by hunting and trading birds. As more farmers turned the birds' habitat into cropland, the number of game birds decreased. It became necessary to license hunters. People learned that it was important to control the number of birds they took from nature.

Due to widespread hunting and loss of habitat, some kinds of birds did not survive. For example, the passenger pigeon became **extinct** in 1914. The trumpeter swan, bald eagle, and wild turkey were close to dying out until laws were made to protect them.

After the Civil War, U.S. Army officer George Armstrong Custer had various duties until he died in a battle against American Indians. Among these duties was leading officials into new U.S. territories. He took people such as Russia's Grand Duke Alexi Alexandrovich hunting for game birds and other animals.

TIMELINE

64,000 years ago
Bows and arrows were used in Africa.

4,000 years ago
Raptors were used in China to help hunt other birds.

240 years ago
Reloadable small firearms came into use, first in warfare and soon after in hunting.

over 130 years ago
Pheasants were first brought to North America from Asia.

almost 80 years ago
In 1934, the U.S. Congress passed the Migratory Bird Hunting Stamp Act to help raise money for bird **conservation** programs.

Birds

Tracking

Birds are most active in the morning and evening, so these are the best times for hunting. Finding birds can be tricky. Most animals leave tracks that a hunter can follow. Birds leave some tracks, but they spend much of their time in the air. This means that a bird hunter often cannot follow tracks to find prey. Instead, the hunter must learn which habitat a type of bird prefers. He or she needs to know what bushes, trees, grasses, or reeds the bird likes. The hunter also needs to know what food the bird eats.

An upland bird hunter must search carefully. Upland birds are **camouflaged** in the brush. A waterfowl hunter must choose a pond or lake with the right habitat and food. Then, the hunter waits for the birds to appear. Birds often show up suddenly overhead or fly out of the brush with a great deal of noise. The hunter must remain calm to make a steady shot.

A blind is any type of cover a hunter uses to remain hidden.

Finding Birds

A hunter must recognize the **species** of bird by its color, wings, and the way it flies. To be successful, the hunter must know about the habits and habitat of each kind of game bird. Sometimes, the hunter will have only a second or two to identify the bird.

Canada Goose
Canada geese are found around ponds, lakes, and rivers.

Mallard
Mallards live in wetlands such as marshes and streams.

Pheasant
Pheasants can live in wetlands or in dry fields.

Wild Turkey
Wild turkeys use forested areas for cover.

Wood Duck
Wood ducks like to stay in areas alongside rivers.

Birds

Equipment and Clothing

A common tool for bird hunting is the 12-gauge shotgun. A gauge is a unit used to measure a gun barrel. The barrel is the main tube of a gun. Other tools include **decoys** and **duck calls**. A hunter floats decoys on the water and uses a duck call when the birds fly by. Waterfowl hunters sometimes use a blind. This fence-like structure is often covered by nets of dried grass. A blind can hide both hunters and dogs.

What to Wear

Waterproof Boots

Camouflage Gloves

Hat

Blaze Orange Vest

Outdoor Hunting Guide

Bird hunters often use trained dogs, called gun dogs. A "pointer" dog will freeze when it smells birds in the brush. The dog's nose points to where the birds are. A "flusher" dog will wait until the hunter is ready and then scare the birds, so that they fly into the air. For hunting waterfowl, a "retriever" can be trained to get a bird from the water.

In some states and provinces, upland bird hunters must wear bright orange clothing. The color is often called blaze orange. It helps other hunters see a hunter in the brush. Turkey hunters often wear camouflage clothing. Good shoes or boots are important as well. They protect the foot from injury. Waterfowl hunters need high boots, called hip boots or waders, to keep dry in the water.

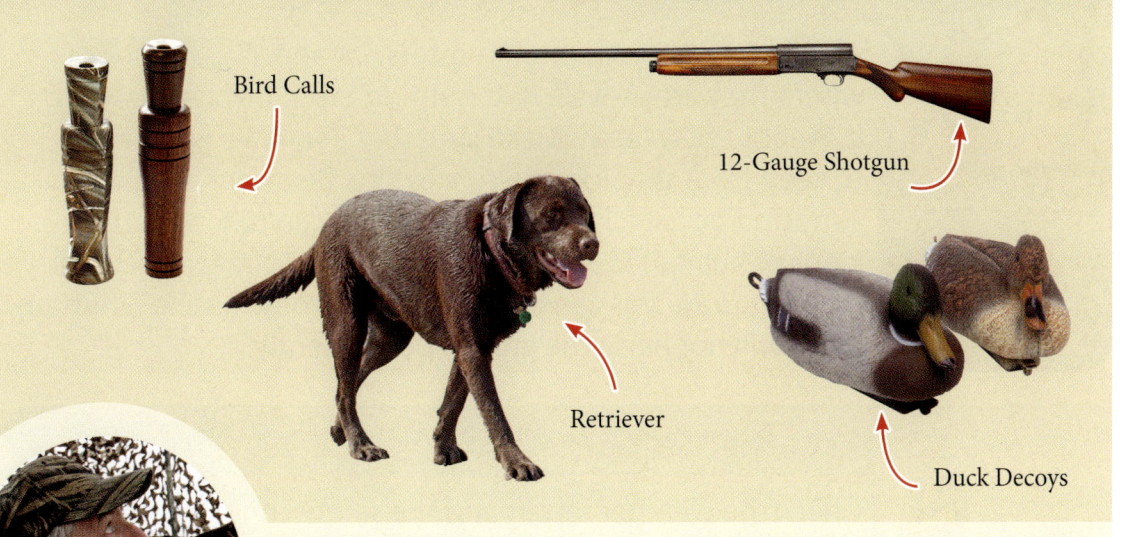

Tools of the Trade

Bird Calls

12-Gauge Shotgun

Retriever

Duck Decoys

HUNTING TECHNOLOGY Electronic duck calls use the recorded sounds of real ducks to help a hunter trick ducks into thinking other ducks are nearby. The hunter can choose from several sounds, such as the sound of a distant greeting, of a lonely female, or of ducks feeding. The device uses batteries and weighs less than 2 pounds (0.9 kg).

Safety

Bird hunters need to hunt safely. There are several things to remember in order to keep safe while bird hunting. Here are some basic safety tips.

Firearm Safety

A firearm should fit the hunter well. It should not be too large. Keep firearms pointed in a safe direction at all times. Treat every firearm as if it is loaded. Keep your finger off the **trigger guard** until you are ready to shoot. Keep the gun's safety on until you are ready to fire. The safety is a type ofdevice. It helps to stop accidental firings.

Environmental Safety

Always know where other hunters are and, if using dogs, where they are as well. Bird hunting often involves walking in wet or rocky areas. Make sure that you have good boots to keep from slipping and to stay dry. Be aware of your surroundings at all times. Bird hunters can run into other kinds of animals that may be dangerous. Some hunters carry pepper spray. This can stop an animal from chasing a hunter, but it will not harm the animal permanently.

Weather Safety

Check the weather report and fire safety conditions before heading out to hunt. Dress in layers to be prepared for different weather conditions. Carry an emergency blanket, a flashlight, and a first aid kit, to be prepared for a change in the weather or an accident. Bring matches and lighters, in case you need to start a fire. Bring extra food and water, in case your trip turns out to be longer than planned.

Safety in Numbers

It is safer to hunt with at least one other person. Accidents can happen. If someone gets hurt, someone else is needed to help or call for help. Hunting parties should let other people know when they are leaving and where they are going. Hunters should tell others when to expect a return.

Be Sure of the Target

Always know your target before you shoot. Know what is in front of your target and what is behind it. Do not shoot at targets too close to roads or farms, where there may be other animals or people. Protect yourself as well. Wearing blaze orange clothing allows a hunter to be seen more easily.

HUNTER CHECKLIST

1. necessary paperwork, including a license, duck stamp, and hunter education card
2. blaze orange clothing item
3. firearm
4. ammunition
5. flashlight
6. batteries
7. cell phone
8. Global Positioning System (GPS) device, map, and compass
9. binoculars
10. knife
11. small handsaw
12. 50 feet (15 m) of nylon rope
13. water
14. first aid kit
15. small mirror
16. whistle

Track the FACTS

- A major cause of accidents is "swinging on game." This means a hunter shoots over a wide area. Shooting wide increases the chance of hitting another hunter.
- Another frequent cause of accidents is failure to identify the target.
- More accidents happen when people are bird hunting than when they are hunting big game or small game.

Birds 15

Responsible hunters do not allow their dogs to leave them and run on private land.

Hunting Responsibly

In 1934, the U.S. government passed a law to protect waterfowl and wetlands. Now, waterfowl hunters must buy a Federal Migratory Bird Hunting and Conservation Stamp. This is often called the duck stamp. The duck stamp is a permit to hunt birds. Each hunter must carry a signed stamp when hunting. The sale of these stamps has raised more than $750 million to protect 5.3 million acres (2.1 million hectares) of duck habitat.

Hunters, bird-watchers, and collectors buy the stamps. Each year, artists compete to have their designs chosen for the duck stamp. In Canada, hunters must buy a similar stamp. It can be used in all provinces and territories. Each state or province allows bird hunting at certain times of year. This helps to keep the number of birds under control. Having too many birds can destroy the habitat and threaten other living things.

Before shooting, a hunter should study the area behind and around the target.

An agreement between the United States, Canada, and Mexico protects birds that travel through these countries. The agreement states where and when these birds can be hunted. It also sets a bag limit. This is the number of birds a hunter is allowed to shoot.

Hunters must be aware that their activities affect other animals and people. Laws require waterfowl hunters to use certain kinds of shot, which are the tiny balls shot from the gun. Lead shot cannot be used because it poisons birds, fish, and other animals. People who eat animals shot with lead could become sick.

Bird Hunting Careers

Gun Dog Trainer
A gun dog trainer must enjoy working with dogs. A trainer will teach dogs how to handle a bird without damaging it. Dogs may be trained for specific jobs, such as flushing game. They can be taught to track or retrieve game. A very talented dog may be trained to do all three. There is no formal schooling to become a gun dog trainer. The trainers learn from one another. Entering competitions can help a trainer become better known.

Birds 17

The Rules

Poaching means hunting at a time or place where it is not allowed. For example, hunting from a moving car or boat is usually against the law. So is hunting for birds at night. Poaching can also mean hunting without a license, taking more birds than allowed, or hunting unfairly. The punishment for bird poaching is usually a fine, which may be different in each state or province.

Understanding the rules includes knowing the number of birds that can be captured.

In most states, waterfowl hunters need to paste their federal duck stamp and a state duck stamp to their licenses. Canada requires a Canadian duck stamp. In addition, U.S. bird hunters have to register with the Harvest Information Program. This group finds out what people are hunting and where. The information helps governments decide which birds should be protected and which can be hunted more.

Sportsmanship is an important part of hunting. Being a good sport takes many forms. It is not illegal to shoot ducks that are sitting or swimming, but it is not sportsmanlike. Most hunters enjoy the challenge of shooting a bird in flight. Some make the hunt even more challenging by using a bow and arrow.

Conservation rangers teach hunter education classes.

Track the FACTS

- A hunter can use a bird of prey, such as a falcon, a hawk, or an eagle, to hunt waterfowl and upland birds. This is called falconry.
- There are six different species of quail to be hunted. They are the California quail, mountain quail, Gambel's quail, scaled quail, bobwhite quail, and Mearns's quail. Up to 1.2 million California quails are shot each year in the state of California.

Birds 19

After the Hunt

A hunter may wish to keep a bird as a trophy. Pheasants and some species of ducks are very colorful. Some people prefer to preserve that beauty and display it. A **taxidermist** can create a trophy by stuffing the animal and mounting it for display.

The feathers of some birds are used to make imitation flies, used to attract fish while fishing. Most game birds, however, are hunted for food. First, the bird's feathers are plucked. Then, the bird is prepared for cooking. The flavor that a cooked bird has depends in part on what it has been eating.

Glazed Roast Pheasant

Ingredients
1 pheasant
¼ cup (68 grams) salt
4 cups (950 milliliters) water
2 whole carrots or stalks of celery
1 teaspoon (3 g) ground red pepper
¼ cup (60 ml) maple or fruit syrup

Directions
1. Place the bird in a glass dish. Dissolve the salt in the water, and pour the liquid over the bird. Cover and refrigerate for 5 to 6 hours.
2. Preheat the oven to 450° Fahrenheit (230° Celsius). Remove the bird from the refrigerator, and pat it dry. Place the carrots or celery stalks a few inches apart in the middle of a roasting pan.
3. Sprinkle the bird with ground red pepper and place it on the carrots.
4. Roast the bird for 20 minutes. Turn the temperature down to 375°F (190°C) and continue roasting for 20 more minutes.
5. Turn the bird over, and drizzle the syrup over it. Continue roasting and basting with syrup for 20 to 30 minutes. Watch carefully, as the syrup may burn.
6. The pheasant is done when the temperature in the thigh is 160°F (70°C).
7. Remove the bird from the roasting pan, and allow it to cool on a cutting board for 10 minutes.
8. Then, carve the bird, and enjoy.

Game Bird Report

Now, it is your turn to go to work. Choose one of the birds listed on page 7 of this book. Using this book, your school or local library, and the internet, write a report about hunting this animal.

Research tips:
Look for additional books about bird hunting in your library under the Dewey Decimal System number 799.

Useful search terms for the internet include "bird hunting" plus the name of your state or province, "tracking birds," "quail," or any other bird you have selected.

Key questions to answer:
1. What type of bird is it, and why is it hunted?
2. What is its habitat?
3. What tools, clothing, and equipment are used to hunt this bird?
4. Are there rules and regulations, including bag limits, for hunting in your area?
5. What licenses or stamps are required?
6. During what season and time of day can you hunt this bird?

Birds 21

Take Aim Quiz

1 What is another name for bird hunting?

2 What is a male pheasant called?

3 What North American bird became extinct because of hunting and habitat loss?

4 What kind of dog freezes when it smells a bird?

5 Who hides in a blind when hunting?

6 For what purpose is the money from duck stamps used?

7 Why is it illegal to use lead shot when hunting?

8 What is hunting without a license called?

ANSWERS
1. fowling 2. rooster 3. passenger pigeon 4. pointer 5. waterfowl hunters 6. conservation projects 7. It is poisonous. 8. poaching

Key Words

brush: a dense growth of bushes

camouflaged: colored to blend in with the surroundings

conservation: the protection and careful use of forests, rivers, minerals, and other natural resources

decoys: living or artificial animals used to attract other animals within hunting range

duck calls: instruments that imitate the sounds ducks make

extinct: no longer living in the world

habitats: the places where an animal or a plant lives or grows

migrate: to move from one place to another in response to weather or other changes

muzzle-loaded: loaded by pushing the gunpowder in the forward part of the gun

range: the farthest possible distance, such as the distance a gun can shoot

raptors: birds that eat the meat of other animals

species: groups of individuals with common characteristics

sportsmanship: the practice or act of behaving fairly

taxidermist: a person who prepares, stuffs, and mounts animals for display

trigger guard: a metal or plastic loop around the trigger to help keep the gun from firing

trophy: a record-setting animal or souvenir of a hunt

Index

bow and arrow 5, 8, 9, 19
Canada goose 6, 7, 11
conservation 9, 16, 19, 22
decoy 12, 13
dog 12, 13, 14, 16, 17, 22
dove 7
duck call 12, 13
equipment 12, 13, 21
feathers 6, 8, 20
food 4, 6, 9, 10, 14, 20
fowling 4, 22
gun dog trainer 17
habitat 4, 6, 9, 10, 11, 16, 17, 21, 22
license 5, 9, 15, 18, 19, 21, 22
mallard 7, 11
pheasant 4, 6, 7, 9, 11, 20, 22
poaching 18, 22
quail 4, 6, 8, 19, 21
safety 5, 14, 15
shotgun 8, 12, 13
sport 4, 5, 19
teal 7
turkey 4, 6, 9, 11, 13
waterfowl 6, 7, 8, 10, 12, 13, 16, 17, 19, 22
wood duck 11

Log on to www.av2books.com

AV² by Weigl brings you media enhanced books that support active learning. Go to www.av2books.com, and enter the special code found on page 2 of this book. You will gain access to enriched and enhanced content that supplements and complements this book. Content includes video, audio, weblinks, quizzes, a slide show, and activities.

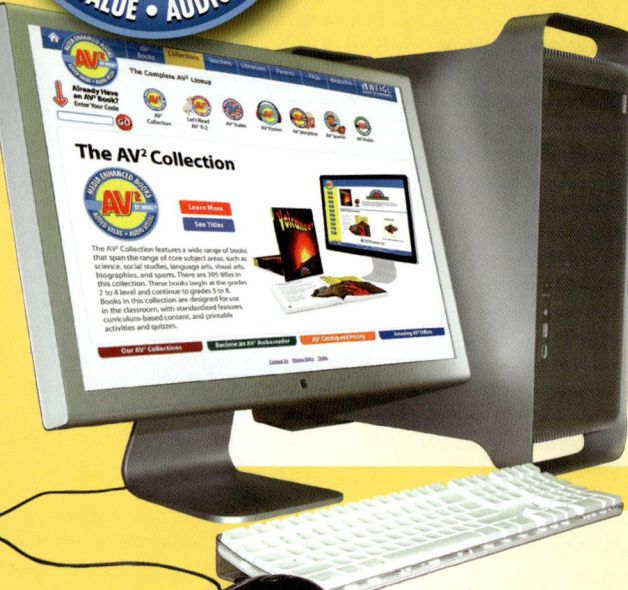

Audio
Listen to sections of the book read aloud.

Video
Watch informative video clips.

Embedded Weblinks
Gain additional information for research.

Try This!
Complete activities and hands-on experiments.

WHAT'S ONLINE?

Try This!	Embedded Weblinks	Video	EXTRA FEATURES
Complete a tracking activity. Identify game birds. Try this matching activity for bird hunting equipment. Test your knowledge of bird hunting.	Learn more about bird hunting. Find the bird hunting rules for your state. Read more about hunting safety.	Watch a video about bird hunting. Watch a video about game birds.	**Audio** Listen to sections of the book read aloud. **Key Words** Study vocabulary, and complete a matching word activity. **Slide Show** View images and captions, and prepare a presentation **Quizzes** Test your knowledge.

AV² was built to bridge the gap between print and digital. We encourage you to tell us what you like and what you want to see in the future.

Sign up to be an AV² Ambassador at www.av2books.com/ambassador.

Due to the dynamic nature of the Internet, some of the URLs and activities provided as part of AV² by Weigl may have changed or ceased to exist. AV² by Weigl accepts no responsibility for any such changes. All media enhanced books are regularly monitored to update addresses and sites in a timely manner. Contact AV² by Weigl at 1-866-649-3445 or av2books@weigl.com with any questions, comments, or feedback.

AUG 2 2 2012